Ode to my Youth:

And Other Thoughts

By: Kaitlyn Rose

Ode to my Youth: And Other Thoughts

Self-published using Amazon Kindle Direct Publishing

ISBN: 979-8-9898290-1-9

First Edition: December 2023

Cover Artwork By: Plan B Studios

MY YOUNGER SELF

I think a lot about who I used to be, my younger self. There are so many things I wish I could go back in time and tell her:

He is going to break your heart, tread lightly

Not all friendships last forever. People grow apart and that's okay.

Failure is not a dirty word.

Sometimes seeing the best in people doesn't work out.

People aren't judging you nearly as much as you think they are.

You don't always get closure.

Some people just won't like you, no matter what you do. Let it go.

But experience is the best teacher, words of wisdom wouldn't have been enough.

She needed to experience each and every one of those things to become the person I see when I look in the mirror today.

OUR FIRST KISS

I had confessed my feelings for you a while
 ago

But you brushed them off until tonight

You looked into my eyes

Confirmed my feelings were reciprocated

My heart skipped a beat in that moment

You leaned in and kissed me

Slowly

Intently

*It's been 8 years since that night and I still
 remember the taste of coffee on your
 lips*

BURN

The fire is raging

The warmth envelopes my skin

The flames are dancing

Inviting me closer

Closer

I know I shouldn't

But the heat feels too good

I step forward and reach out

I feel it burn

UPPERHAND

I was an adult but just barely

Time and experience were on your side

You saw my naivety and took it as opportunity

LESSONS

You were the hardest lesson I had to learn

A NATURAL

I still think about all the lies you told

How easy the words just rolled off your
    tongue

Why did it come so naturally to you?

THIEF

You knew better and you did it anyway

I'll never forgive you for stealing my youth

CHAMELEON

Somewhere down the line I realized

I wasn't what you were looking for

I changed into different versions of myself

In hopes of swaying you

Everchanging to be who you wanted me to
be

To be enough

No matter how hard I tried

You never saw me the way I saw you

ENDLESS

Sometimes I wonder how many tears I've
    cried over you

HEROIN

Your love was like heroin

Coursing through my veins

I became addicted from the very first kiss

The rush was indescribable

I'd never felt anything quite like it

Pure euphoria

I craved you

I couldn't focus on anything or anyone else

I was blind to your side effects

Always itching for my next fix of you

You were slowly killing me

I didn't care

I needed the high I felt when you were near
me

But every moment I spent with you

I lost a piece of myself

Until all that was left

Was the shell of who I used to be

LUNCH

We were having lunch like any other normal day

Yet today was anything but normal

You mentioned she had moved out

You were finally free

Five years later and we both were available fully

We could finally be together like I'd been fantasizing about since the start

All this time had gone by

I hoped and dreamed things could be different

Now they were

I waited for you to pull me in and say

It's you and me now

But you didn't

I waited and waited

And after years of waiting, I realized

That was never what you wanted

THE LAST TIME

You never know when you'll be seeing someone for the last time...

OUR LAST ENCOUNTER

I was vulnerable

My life had just crumbled before me

I was grasping on to you

The one person I needed in that moment

We shared dinner and tears and my bed

You left in a hurry right after

Another call from her

You got dressed and started to leave

You turned to me with apologetic eyes

Kissed me quickly and disappeared out the
    door

I haven't seen you since

CLOSURE

You don't always get closure

You'll be forced to move on

With so many questions left unanswered

DROWNING

Enough time has passed

The tears no longer fall

But I think a lot about them

Tears that could fill swimming pools, lakes,
and oceans

*I'll be forever drowning in what could have
been*

ENDINGS

An ending is simply a way to make room for another beginning

HOPE

I'm thankful for you

You allowed me to feel a love I never knew
    possible

But that love was one-sided

Unrequited

I was someone you ran to in your times of
    need

    When you needed validation

    When you needed an ego boost

    When you needed sex

And although my love was never reciprocated

It allowed me a glimpse into what love could
    be

If I could love as fiercely as I loved you

Someone who was full of conditions

I can only imagine the feeling of having that
    love returned

And I am hopeful

NEW TATTOO

I got a new tattoo today

Just below my left wrist

It's small and simple

A blooming poppy with leaves

A small gesture with a friend I realized holds
    even more meaning

*There is finally a piece of me you will never get
    to know*

BETTER MAN

I sincerely hope you learned

How to treat people better

COULD HAVE BEEN

I am sad

Not because I miss you

But because I miss who I thought you were

And what we could have been

IDENTITY CRISIS

I was so busy chasing you

I never learned who I was or who I wanted to
be

HAPPIER

If you would have told me back then, I never would have believed you...

But I'm happier without you

ANOTHER UNIVERSE

Somewhere in another universe, you and I make it work:

> We meet at the right time
>
> You're a good man with good intentions
>
> There aren't any hurdles in our way

I imagine us in our living room, drinking whiskey and having deep conversation.

I can picture us playing video games before turning on some trash tv and making fun of the contestants on the show.

I see us making dinner together, finding it impossible to keep our hands off each other. Never outgrowing the honeymoon phase even after years together.

We are so in love it makes others around us roll their eyes, wishing deep down they had the same love we have.

In another universe, we got it right

But in this one, I am living life without you.

WILLPOWER

I'm grateful you moved 3,000 miles away

As much as I'd like to think I've moved on

I don't know that I'd have the willpower

To turn you away if you showed up at my door

THE FIRST TIME

I met someone last night

It was the first time since you I felt pretty

It was the first time since you I felt wanted

It was the first time since you I wanted
      someone else

ELECTRICITY

I have still yet to find someone

With lips as electric as yours

DECISIONS

Are you happy with the choices you made?

SINNER

Did you ever confess to her your sins

Or is she still believing your lies?

THE HEAD AND THE HEART

My heart desperately wants to let you go

But my brain cannot seem to forget you

NEW PERSPECTIVE

I've always loved Fall. It's Mother Nature's way of starting anew. The leaves change color and float from the branches. The rain pours from the sky, cleansing the earth. The air is crisp, fresh; nipping at your skin as you step outside.

Endings can be sad; they can be scary. It can feel like there's no coming back from them. But sometimes, as Mother Nature shows us, endings can be beautiful.

The sun comes out again and you remember how amazing the warmth feels on your skin. Flowers bloom from the ground, creating a more colorful world. The same trees that lost their leaves are now blossoming again.

Endings allow the opportunity for something new to happen.

LIGHT SWITCH

If they don't stay with you

During your darkest hour

Do not let them come back

When you've found the light switch

FREE

One day, something just clicked. I wish I could put my finger on the exact moment it happened, but there came a point in my existence where I no longer cared about what others thought of me. Since then, I've lived a much more fulfilling life, free from the shackles of doubt and self-consciousness.

At some point, I sincerely hope you experience this too.

APPROVAL COMES FROM WITHIN

If you consistently seek approval from
everyone you meet

You'll spend your life being sorely
disappointed

HUMAN

We are not robots

It's inevitable

We'll make many mistakes in our lifetime

It's how we learn from them that matters

LETTING GO

Life is just too short to hold on to things not meant for you:

> To that high paying job that leaves you feeling empty and soulless
>
> To the partner who doesn't love you the way you deserve to be loved
>
> To the opinions of others that fill you with doubt

It's time to let go

MY GREATEST FLAW

Why do I keep getting butterflies for the wrong people?

YOU

I sat down today to write something new

But all I could think of were thoughts of you

WONDERING

I wonder if you think of me

When you're drinking your morning coffee

Or when your mind is wandering at work

Or at night when you're trying to fall asleep

Do I ever cross your mind

Like you do mine?

LESSONS LEARNED

I want to confess to you how I feel

How thoughts of you consume my mind

How the best part of my day is talking to you

But I keep it all in

*I've learned the hard way, sometimes things
are better left unsaid*

DREAMING

I've dreamt of you every night this week

Glimpses of a life that will never be

DEAR BFF

I miss you, friend

Our lives have taken very different paths

Paths I thought would intersect much more
often

But I haven't heard from you in six months...

I can't be angry at you for the life you've
chosen

But I get tired of my texts going unnoticed

Tired of the plans that never get made

I miss the way it was when we were younger

SOULMATES

I believe in many different types of soulmates.

I believe in platonic soulmates. Someone who you immediately connect with; someone you love unconditionally. Physical intimacy is not present, but not missed. It is simply the purest and deepest form of friendship one can experience.

I believe in one-sided soulmates. You crave this person; you cannot get enough of this person. Your love runs so deep it simultaneously scares and invigorates you. You are obsessed with everything this person does, who they are. This person does not feel the same way about you. They may have love for you, but it is not with the same conviction as your love for them. This soulmate will break your heart, but teach you so much

I also believe in romantic soulmates. That there is someone out there you are meant to be with, and they are also meant to be with you. You share the same values; you understand each other on such a deep level that it feels like you've known them in another life. Where you connect emotionally, physically, spiritually; this person is your other half, and you theirs.

I am still waiting to find my romantic soulmate, but I believe he exists. I'm no longer trying to force it. What will be, will be.

We will meet when the time is right.

SELF LOVE

I've learned how to love someone else

But I'm still learning

How to love myself

REFLECTION

I want to know what it's like

To look in the mirror and not hate what you
see

CHANGING THE NARRATIVE

I am pretty ~~for a fat girl~~

DAILY AFFIRMATIONS

I am kind

I am warm

I am smart

I am empathetic

I am strong

I am honest

I am accomplished

I am enough

BODY IMAGE

I have had stretch marks and cellulite on various parts of my body for as long as I can remember.

I have seen 150 lbs. and I have seen 250 lbs. I have been a size 8 and I have been a size 18. I have gained the weight and lost the weight more times than I can count.

While my weight has fluctuated over the years, one thing has always stayed the same: I hate the way my body looks.

I've struggled my entire life with my body image, thinking *if I can just lose the weight, I'll be happy*. But then I lose the weight and I'm still not happy.

I desperately want to love my body. She is so powerful and protective. Yet, I don't take care of her like I should. I eat whatever I'm craving, I don't drink nearly enough water, and I haven't exercised in longer than I can remember.

I believe the first step in loving my body is taking better care of it. Not to look better per se, but to *feel* better. Because if I don't feel good on the inside, I can't feel good on the outside.

LIVING WITH ANXIETY

I get jealous of those with normal minds. Those who can fall asleep at night without a worry in the world. Those whose thoughts are never consumed with made up scenarios. Those who process stress in healthy ways versus manifesting it into a panic attack. Those who don't lie awake at 2:00am dwelling on that one idiotic thing they did 5 years and 72 days ago. Those who have never felt the inexplainable sense of impending doom.

I wonder what it's like to have a mind like that.

PANIC ATTACK

I'm holding my breath and flailing my arms

It's triggered my fight or flight

I'm desperately trying not to drown

Yet there isn't any water in sight

DEPRESSION

Sometimes it's sleeping for 14 hours straight

Sometimes it's not washing your hair for a
week

Sometimes it's crying for no reason

Sometimes it's crying for a very specific
reason

Sometimes it's not feeling sad but rather not
feeling anything

Sometimes it's feeling like you've forgotten
how to live

Sometimes it's feeling hopeless

Sometimes it's feeling like life isn't worth
living

To anyone who's also experienced these feelings:

I see you

I'm so glad you're here.

You are not alone

DEFECTIVE

These are the times I feel broken

When my heart and my head aren't listening
    to reason

When I feel like the world is caving in

But everything is perfectly normal

I try to ground myself

I practice my breathing

I remind myself I'm okay

I take medication

But nothing helps it go away

These feelings of panic and anxiety

I know it will get better in time
But I'm suffering in the now

My body feels defective
Can I trade it in for a new one?

SUCCESS

I used to use society's definition of success to determine if I was in an acceptable place in my life. I would always come up short; I had no house, no husband, no children. It made me sad and anxious that I was 'so far behind' in life.

Then, one day, I took a step back and really took stock of what I had and what I've accomplished. I have a good job and make a good salary. I am successfully supporting myself with an apartment and car of my own.

I realized I don't even want a house, or a husband, or even children.

I just want to be happy.

ODE TO MY YOUTH

Oh, sweet girl with your heart on your sleeve

You're still unaware he's going to leave

You don't yet know that your current best
    friend

Will leave you to fend for yourself in the end

Oh, sweet girl I know money's tight

Just know that it's going to be alright

It's okay that you moved back home again

It allowed a new chapter of life to begin

Oh, sweet girl for you my heart breaks

But experiencing it all is what it takes

To become the girl you turn out to be

Because without any of that

You wouldn't be me

www.ingramcontent.com/pod-product-compliance
Lightning Source LLC
Chambersburg PA
CBHW070457050426
42449CB00012B/3006